CHILDREN 92 HOMER 2014
Gagne, Tammy
Homer

11/20/2013

JUNIOR
BIOGRAPHY
FROM
ANCIENT
CIVILIZATIONS

HOMER

TAMMY GAGNE

Mitchell Lane
PUBLISHERS

P.O. Box 196
Hockessin, Delaware 19707
Visit us on the web: www.mitchelllane.com
Comments? Email us: mitchelllane@mitchelllane.com

JUNIOR
BIOGRAPHY
FROM
ANCIENT
CIVILIZATIONS

Alexander the Great • Archimedes
Augustus Caesar • Confucius • Genghis Khan
Homer • Leif Erikson • Marco Polo
Nero • Socrates

ABOUT THE AUTHOR: Tammy Gagne is the author of numerous books for adults and children, including *A Kid's Guide to the Voting Process*, *Life on the Reservations*, and *Augustus Caesar* for Mitchell Lane Publishers. She resides in northern New England with her husband and son. One of her favorite pastimes is visiting schools to speak to kids about the writing process.

PUBLISHER'S NOTE: The facts on which the story in this book is based have been thoroughly researched. Documentation of such research can be found on pages 44–45. While every possible effort has been made to ensure accuracy, the publisher will not assume liability for damages caused by inaccuracies in the data, and makes no warranty on the accuracy of the information contained herein.

Printing 1   2   3   4   5   6   7   8   9

Library of Congress
Cataloging-in-Publication Data

Gagne, Tammy.
 Homer / by Tammy Gagne.
    pages cm. — (Junior Biography from Ancient Civilizations)
 Includes bibliographical references and index.
  ISBN 978-1-61228-435-4 (library bound)
1. Homer—Juvenile literature. 2. Poets, Greek—Biography—Juvenile literature. 3. Civilization, Homeric—Juvenile literature. 4. Mythology, Greek, in literature—Juvenile literature. I. Title.
 PA4037.G35 2014
 883'.01—dc23

                                    2013012555

eBook ISBN: 9781612284972

                                          PLB

CONTENTS

Phonetic pronunciations of words in **bold**
can be found on page 46.

Through the centuries many painters have brought Homer and his poems to life through art. "Homer Dictating to a Clerk" dates from 1663. It is by Dutch artist Rembrandt Harmenszoon van Rijn (1606–1669). It hangs in the Mauritshuis, the Royal Picture Gallery in the Netherlands.

The Original Action-Adventure Experience

The setting is the Trojan War, the battle of the invading Greeks against the Trojans that has lasted for 10 years. It is said to have been fought over Helen, the most beautiful woman in the entire world. Helen is married to King **Menelaus*** of Sparta, but she was kidnapped by Paris, the prince of Troy. Her abduction caused Menelaus to seek the help of his fellow Greeks. Under the leadership of Menelaus's brother **Agamemnon**, the Greeks spent two years assembling a fleet of more than 1,000 ships and 100,000 men, then set sail to Troy. Their goal: return the queen to her rightful home.

Although this may sound like the plot outline of a feature film that could be playing in a theater right now, it is actually a story that was written many centuries before movies ever existed. It is called *The Iliad*, and it has been retold many times since its creation. It has indeed been made into several films. But its original form was a poem.

It begins, "Sing, O goddess, the anger of **Achilles** son of Peleus, that brought countless ills

*For pronunciations of words in **bold**, see page 46.

"Paris Abducting Helen" was painted by Scottish artist Gavin Hamilton (1723–1798). It hangs in the Pushkin State Museum of Fine Arts in Moscow, Russia. It depicts Paris, the prince of Troy, kidnapping Helen, the wife of King Menelaus.

upon the **Achaeans**. Many a brave soul did it send hurrying down to Hades, and many a hero did it yield a prey to dogs and vultures, for so were the counsels of Jove fulfilled from the day on which the son of Atreus [Agamemnon], king of men, and great Achilles, first fell out with one another."[1]

Achilles is the hero of *The Iliad*. He is the best warrior in the Greek army. But the Trojans are protected by strong walls and the Greeks can do little except besiege them. During the long siege,

"The Rage of Achilles" was created by Italian painter Giovanni Battista Tiepolo (1696–1770). It hangs in the Villa Valmarana in Vicenza, Italy. Author Terence Hawkins penned a novel about the Trojan War by this same title in 2009.

Achilles wins the love of a woman named **Briseis**. However, Agamemnon takes Briseis from him. Achilles is furious and refuses to fight any longer. When his good friend Patroclos is killed fighting in his place, Achilles is overcome with anger. This anger leads him back to fight against the Trojans. In the end Achilles kills Hector, the best Trojan warrior and Paris's brother.

"The Triumph of Achilles" was painted by Austrian artist Franz von Matsch (1861–1942).

This poem is unlike any other one. For starters, it is extremely long—more than 15,000 lines in all. It is divided into 24 chapters. Because it is so long, *The Iliad* is called an epic poem.

The Iliad is said to have been written by a man named Homer. Many people think that Homer was born in a Greek colony on the coast of Asia Minor, which today is part of the country of Turkey. For many years his birthdate was thought to be around 1200 BCE. Today most scholars believe that this time period marks the date of the war Homer wrote about, rather than the time when he actually lived.

In addition to *The Iliad*, Homer wrote *The Odyssey*. This epic poem tells the tale of the Greek hero **Odysseus** and his 10-year journey back to his home on the Greek island of Ithaca following the Trojan War. Like *The Iliad*, *The Odyssey* is a thrilling story. Odysseus encounters all sorts of unusual and dangerous beings—including a one-eyed giant, cannibals, and sea monsters. The word "odyssey" has come to mean an especially exciting adventure.

The Odyssey is also very long, though not quite as long as *The Iliad*. It is made up of more than 12,000 lines. Like *The Iliad*, it is divided into 24 chapters.

Both *The Iliad* and *The Odyssey* were written in what is known as dactylic hexameter. In this form of poetry, each line of the poem contains between 12 and 17 syllables. These syllables are divided into six groups, or feet ("hex" means six). There is also a very specific rhythm in dactylic hexameter. This rhythm is achieved by combining long and short syllables within each foot. The first syllable of each foot is emphasized, or stressed, and the next one or two are not. For example, the opening line of *The Iliad* would be read like this: SING, o /GODdess, the /ANGer of a/CHILLes /SON of /PEleus.[2]

For such an early time in history, Homer's epics are considered very advanced forms of poetry. Reading them more than once is necessary to completely understand them. Homer may have written other poems during his lifetime, but *The Iliad* and *The Odyssey* are the only ones that have survived.

Strong Women

In ancient Greece, men were regarded as smarter and more powerful than women. This idea is illustrated in *The Iliad*, which represents women as little more than attractive possessions. Helen is stolen from Menelaus by Paris, while Briseis is *taken* from Achilles by Agamemnon.

The Odyssey, however, features many intelligent, strong female characters. **Calypso** is a goddess-nymph who captures Odysseus. She holds him prisoner on her island for seven years. When **Zeus**, the king of the gods, finally forces her to let Odysseus go, Calypso still has power over Odysseus. She convinces him that letting him go was actually her idea. Circe is a goddess-enchantress

William Hamilton (1751–1801), cousin to Gavin Hamilton, painted "Calypso Receiving Telemachus and Mentor in the Grotto."

who turns Odysseus's men into swine to keep him from continuing on his journey. Even Penelope, Odysseus' wife, shows great strength by waiting 20 years for Odysseus to return home.

The strongest female character, though, is **Athena**. This goddess of wisdom has the biggest influence on Odysseus and his story. She saves him from the anger of the sea-god **Poseidon**, convinces his son Telemachus to stop suitors from marrying his mother while his father is away, and keeps Odysseus from giving up on his long journey home.

"Homer and His Guide" by French artist William-Adolphe Bouguereau (1825–1905) can be seen at the Milwaukee Art Museum in Wisconsin. No one knows for sure whether Homer was indeed blind. Most painters and sculptors depicted him this way, because it is such a common belief.

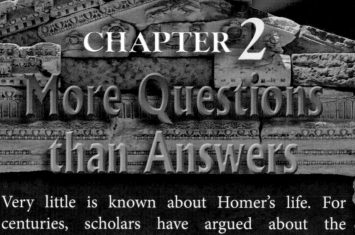

CHAPTER 2
More Questions than Answers

Very little is known about Homer's life. For centuries, scholars have argued about the information that has been passed down about him. When was he born? Where did he live? Where did he get his gift for storytelling? Did he even write the poems himself? No one can be certain of the answers to these questions. Although he wrote some of the longest poems in history, he revealed next to nothing about himself in them. Yet the poems do offer significant clues, both about Homer himself and the times in which he lived.

Many scholars believe that Homer probably lived around 750–700 BCE. One of the reasons for this belief is based on the words he used in his poems. The Greek language was spoken throughout what is now modern-day Greece and the surrounding area, but each region had its own dialect that developed over time. The main dialect used in both *The Iliad* and *The Odyssey* was Ionian Greek. This detail makes it very likely that Homer was from Ionia, which consists of some of the islands in the eastern part of the Aegean Sea

THRACIAN

ILLYRIAN   MACEDONIAN

Chalcidice

Lemnos

● Troy

EPIRUS   Larissa ●   Aegean Sea ●   AEOLIA   ASIA

Corcyra   Dodona ●   MINOR
          THESSALY   Lesbos ● Pergamum

Ambracia

Skyros

Leucas   EUBOEA   LYDIAN
          Delphi ● BOEOTIA ● Chalkis   ● Smyrna
                   Thebes   Chios

Cephallonia   ACHAEA   Megara ● ATTICA   IONIA
          ELIA   Corinth ● Athens   Samos ● ● Ephesus
Zacynthos Olympia ARGOLIS   Andros
          ARCADIA Argos ●   ● Miletus
                   ● Epidaurus   CARIAN

MESSENIA Sparta   CYCLADES
Pylos ●   LACONIA   Naxos

                                              Kos

Thera

Rhodes

CRETE   CYPRUS

For thousands of years, people have tried to pinpoint the exact settings of both *The Iliad* and *The Odyssey*. The locations might have been actual places in ancient Greece—or they may have been based on a combination of locations Homer visited during his lifetime.

and the colonies that dotted the coastline of Asia Minor. *The Iliad* in particular is filled with words in common use during this time period.

Since Homer's work does include other dialects, though, he is thought to have been a traveling bard. In addition to being storytellers, most bards were musicians. They moved from place to place, reciting their poems to their attentive audiences while playing harp-like instruments like the lyre. The music helped set the mood of the stories, much like movie soundtracks make films more exciting today.

According to many legends about Homer, he was blind. Many sculptures of Homer show him with his eyes closed. This belief in his blindness has been passed down since ancient times, but no one knows if it is true. He may have been born blind, he may have lost his sight at some point during his life, or he may have never been blind at all. Many bards were indeed blind. Some people think that being blind gave these storytellers a special gift for being able to *see* things that ordinary people could not. It is also possible that people thought Homer was blind simply because he closed his eyes when reciting his poems. Many modern-day poets and singers close their eyes when they perform. Doing so allows them to ignore the distractions around them and focus entirely on their work instead.

Some people believe that evidence for Homer's blindness comes from a character in *The Odyssey* named **Tiresias**. He is a blind bard who sings about the fall of Troy, and Homer may have been describing himself.

Another reason some people think that Homer was blind relates to colors. In both *The Iliad* and *The Odyssey*, he rarely mentions specific colors. When he does, his descriptions are a bit confusing. Some people even think he talks about colors as if he had never seen them. The phrase "wine-dark sea," for example, is used dozens of times in *The Odyssey*. Wine comes in many colors, but the blue of the sea isn't one of them.

Some scholars point out that Homer uses this phrase most often when he is talking about dark and gloomy weather. Others think that Homer's "wine-dark" phrase describes the depth of the color, not the color itself. American poet Robert Fitzgerald, who translated *The Iliad* and *The Odyssey* in addition to a number of other famous Greek works, has said that he sees Homer's sea as so intense that it looks like a bowl of dye. "The depth of hue of the water was like the depth of hue of a good red wine," he wrote. "So I associate the expression with the richness of hue rather than a specific color. I've been content with that as my personal interpretation."[1]

German artist Carl Ludwig Friedrich Becker (1820–1900) painted "Homer Singing in the Company of Young Greeks." The work shows how enthralled the ancient Greek people were with Homer's poems.

On the other hand, Homer's work often describes scenes of action with enormous detail. This amount of detail would have been very difficult—if not impossible—to show if he was sightless. He may have simply lost his sight late in life as a natural effect of old age. This idea would explain how he was able to write about things that most of us could describe only if we had actually seen them ourselves. It might even help to explain why his sense of color was a bit askew. Perhaps he had remembered colors differently than they really were.

A Theory of Many Homers

Scholars have many theories about Homer. One is that his poems were actually the work of many different people. Those who subscribe to this belief see Homer as a combination of all these people, a legend that people have created over time.

Experts have been studying Homer's works for centuries. As early as the third century BCE, some scholars began insisting that *The Iliad* and *The Odyssey* are much too different to have been written by the same person. *The Iliad*, for example, includes more old-fashioned words than *The Odyssey*. *The Iliad* also repeats certain phrases over and over, whereas *The Odyssey* does not.

Engraved frontispiece of a 1660 edition of Homer's *The Iliad*

For many readers, the question of one or many Homers isn't important. Author Madeline Miller said, "We still don't know if Homer was one person or many people, whether he was truly the blind bard of legend or someone more prosaic. What we do know is that when these poems were written they were intended not just for an elite audience, but for everyone ... Whoever created these gorgeous poems, I owe them a huge debt of gratitude. Almost 3,000 years later they are as fresh as they ever were."[2]

In "Portrait of Homer" the bard holds a piece of paper listing the names of the cities that claim to be his birthplace. Homer's origin isn't the only mystery here. No one knows for certain who painted this piece. It is believed to be the work of a Flemish artist, though.

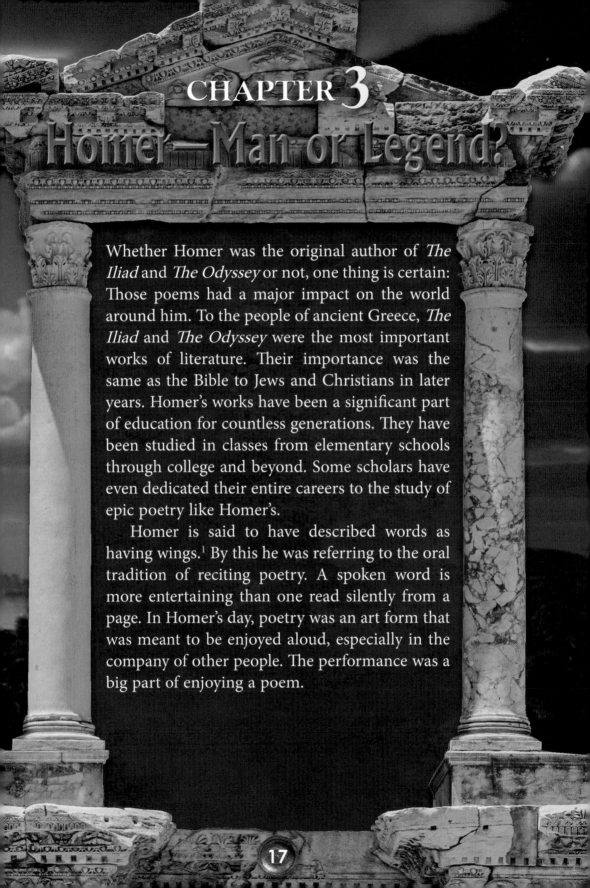

CHAPTER 3
Homer—Man or Legend?

Whether Homer was the original author of *The Iliad* and *The Odyssey* or not, one thing is certain: Those poems had a major impact on the world around him. To the people of ancient Greece, *The Iliad* and *The Odyssey* were the most important works of literature. Their importance was the same as the Bible to Jews and Christians in later years. Homer's works have been a significant part of education for countless generations. They have been studied in classes from elementary schools through college and beyond. Some scholars have even dedicated their entire careers to the study of epic poetry like Homer's.

Homer is said to have described words as having wings.[1] By this he was referring to the oral tradition of reciting poetry. A spoken word is more entertaining than one read silently from a page. In Homer's day, poetry was an art form that was meant to be enjoyed aloud, especially in the company of other people. The performance was a big part of enjoying a poem.

One of France's best-known works depicting Homer is "Homère." It was painted by Jean-Baptiste Auguste Leloir (1809-1892). The piece hangs in the Louvre in Paris.

Around the time of Homer's birth, the Greeks were just beginning to use a written alphabet. Homer is believed to be the first person to record the tales told in *The Iliad* and *The Odyssey*. Even if this is a fact, however, it is unlikely that he created the stories or even all the words all on his own. He probably recorded the poems after hearing them from other bards. Even if he wasn't their original author, he

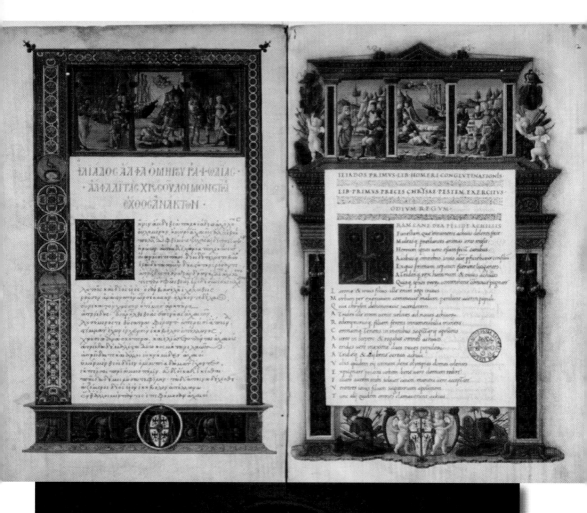

Over the centuries, many people have written translations of Homer's two epics. Seen here is a codex, an early form of a book, that dates back to 1477. The left page shows the Greek text of *The Iliad* by Johannes Rossos, while the right page has the corresponding Latin text by Bartolomeo San Vito. The illustrations are by an Italian artist whose identity is unknown. Rossos and San Vito also produced a companion version of *The Odyssey.*

almost certainly helped to shape the poems as he composed them in his mind.

In the early 20th century, epic poetry American scholar Milman Parry offered some interesting opinions about Homer. Parry suggested that the stories Homer told had been passed down over time, from one generation to the next. For centuries people had wondered how this could be done with such detail without a written language. Parry had an opinion about this as well. He argued that they were memorized and performed much like a song today. Putting words into a poem or song to remember them better is one form of a mnemonic device.

Parry died unexpectedly in an accident when he was just 33 years old. His associate Albert Lord continued Parry's work. Their research, and research done by other scholars in later years, showed that this kind of oral storytelling was common all around the world at one time or another. It has been found in Africa, Central Asia, and in North America among Native Americans.

Similar bards have been said to live in various parts of the world as recently as the 20th century, such as the *guslari* in Bosnia. Parry and Lord spent a great deal of time searching for one well-known guslar called Cor Huso, who was said to be able to sing for five or six hours without ever stopping. Some people also claimed that Cor Huso was at least 120 years old and could jump 20 paces at the age of 101.[2] Neither Parry nor Lord could ever find anyone who had actually met Cor Huso. Almost certainly he was a legendary figure rather than a real person.

Did Homer's Poems Lead to the Greek Alphabet?

For more than 2,000 years, most people have thought that the Greek alphabet was created to make doing business easier. Written language and numbers helped keep track of both goods and income. Towards the end of the 20th century, however, a professor from the University of Wisconsin suggested a different theory.

Barry Powell wrote a book called *Homer and the Origin of the Greek Alphabet*. In it he stated that the earliest examples of the Greek alphabet are poems. He went as far as to say that the alphabet may have been created for Homer himself, since he was the first Greek poet.

The Greek alphabet was the first to include vowels. Some people think that this was because the Greek language contained many words that began with these letters. Powell, however, thinks that the vowels have more to do with recording of Homer's poetry. "Why would someone be so interested in putting down what the language sounded like," he said, "if the sound of the words weren't important? And where else is the sound of language more important than in poetry."[3]

ΙΛΙΑΣ

Μῆνιν ἄειδε, θεά, Πηληϊάδεω Ἀχιλῆος
οὐλομένην, ἣ μυρί᾽ Ἀχαιοῖς ἄλγε᾽ ἔθηκε,
πολλὰς δ᾽ ἰφθίμους ψυχὰς Ἄϊδι προΐαψεν
ἡρώων, αὐτοὺς δὲ ἑλώρια τεῦχε κύνεσσιν
οἰωνοῖσί τε πᾶσι· Διὸς δ᾽ ἐτελείετο βουλή·
ἐξ οὗ δὴ τὰ πρῶτα διαστήτην ἐρίσαντε
Ἀτρεΐδης τε ἄναξ ἀνδρῶν καὶ δῖος Ἀχιλλεύς.

The beginning of *The Iliad* in its Greek form. The translation is below.

Sing, goddess, the anger of Peleus' son Achilleus and its devastation, which put pains thousandfold upon the Achaians, hurled in their multitudes to the house of Hades strong souls of heroes, but gave their bodies to be the delicate feasting of dogs, of all birds, and the will of Zeus was accomplished since that time when first there stood in division of conflict Atreus' son the lord of men and brilliant Achilleus.

This statue of Homer was created during the 19th century. It stands in St. Petersburg, Russia. In this depiction, the bard is holding a lyre. Many bards played this stringed musical instrument as they recited their poems.

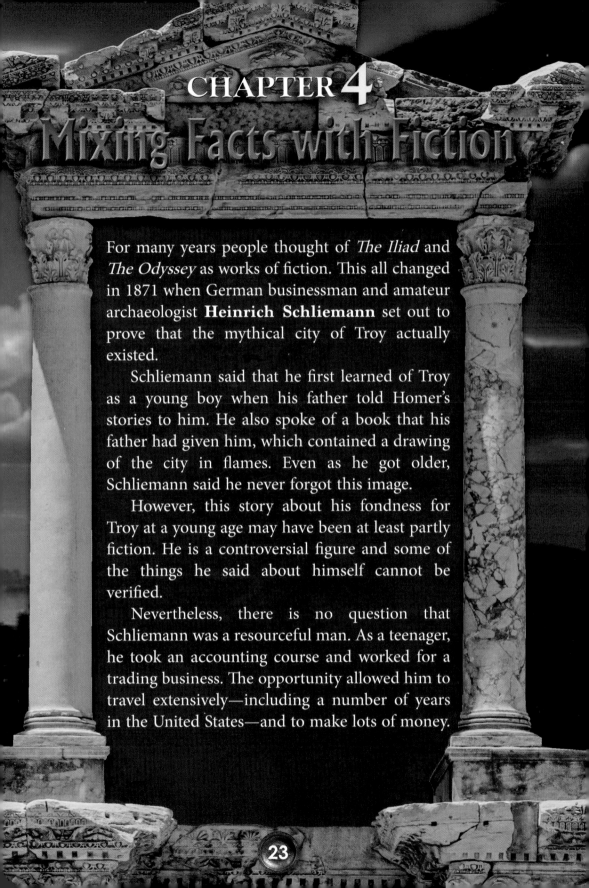

CHAPTER 4
Mixing Facts with Fiction

For many years people thought of *The Iliad* and *The Odyssey* as works of fiction. This all changed in 1871 when German businessman and amateur archaeologist **Heinrich Schliemann** set out to prove that the mythical city of Troy actually existed.

Schliemann said that he first learned of Troy as a young boy when his father told Homer's stories to him. He also spoke of a book that his father had given him, which contained a drawing of the city in flames. Even as he got older, Schliemann said he never forgot this image.

However, this story about his fondness for Troy at a young age may have been at least partly fiction. He is a controversial figure and some of the things he said about himself cannot be verified.

Nevertheless, there is no question that Schliemann was a resourceful man. As a teenager, he took an accounting course and worked for a trading business. The opportunity allowed him to travel extensively—including a number of years in the United States—and to make lots of money.

Heinrich Schliemann, archaeologist in search of Troy

Sophia Schliemann, Heinrich's wife, wearing jewelry found at Hisarlik

By the time he discovered archaeology, Schliemann had collected a sizeable fortune to invest in the search for Troy. He was so committed to finding the city that he ran an advertisement in a Greek newspaper looking for a Greek wife to help him.

Based on information from a British archeologist named Frank Calvert, Schliemann had a strong feeling that Homer's Troy could be found under a Turkish hill called Hisarlik. He was so certain that he wouldn't even wait for permission from the Turkish government to start digging. His impatience was his biggest downfall. When the country finally approved his dig, he went too fast and too far. He hired more than a hundred people to dig—and dig deep. When they reached the remains of a stone wall, Schliemann declared that he had found Troy. He even thought that he had found jewels belonging to the famous Helen.

There are in fact nine different cities buried on top of each other at the Hisarlik site. Schliemann's crew had blasted down the second level. The jewels that Schliemann thought were Helen's were actually hundreds of years older than the time frame of Homer's epic poems. More experienced—and

This funeral mask, also called an Agamemnon Mask, is on display at the National Archaeological Museum in Athens, Greece. It was found in Mycenae by Heinrich Schliemann in 1876 and dates back to the 16th century BCE.

The ruins of Troy make up one of the most famous archaeological sites in the world. The site was first excavated in 1871 by Heinrich Schliemann. Before this time many people questioned whether the city actually existed.

more patient—archaeologists would later learn that Schliemann had the right location, but he had simply dug down too far. It appeared that Homer's Troy was more likely the sixth or seventh oldest city under the hill.

Other settings from Homer's work have also been unearthed. In August 2010, Greek archaeologists uncovered what they believe to be the palace of Odysseus on the island of Ithaca. This discovery has provided a possible indication that Odysseus may have been an actual person.

Just because certain places—and even evidence of specific people—have been discovered, it does not mean that Homer's poems are entirely true. No evidence has ever been found to confirm that Achilles or Helen actually existed, for example.

Many scholars think that Homer's tales are a combination of history and fiction to make the tales more interesting. For example, archaeologists have found evidence that Troy was destroyed by an earthquake, not a war. Eric Cline, a historian and archeologist at George Washington University in Washington, D.C., wrote, "The suggestion is that Homer knew that the city he was describing had been destroyed by an earthquake. But that's not how you want to end your monumental saga—with a whimper. So he concocted this idea of a Trojan horse."[1]

The problem is that *The Iliad* ends before the fall of Troy. So it doesn't have any mention of the Trojan horse. However, the Trojan horse is briefly mentioned in *The Odyssey*. Homer's use of the horse might even be a clue to the truth. Poseidon was a god associated with both horses and earthquakes. Some scholars suggest that Poseidon's role in *The Iliad* was a symbol of what actually happened to the city of Troy.

Cline is among those who see Homer's work as a merging of fact and fiction. "The archaeological and textual evidence indicates that a Trojan war or wars took place, and that Homer chose to write about one or more of them by making it into a great ten-year-long saga."[2]

Even Scientists Consider Homer

Most experts who argue about how much of Homer's stories are true are literary scholars. A few scientists have also offered opinions on the subject. In 2008, physicist Marcelo Magnasco and astronomer Constantino Baikouzis from Rockefeller University in New York City conducted a study on the phases of the moon, constellations, and planets. Using special computer software, they recreated the Greek skies over a 135-year period and compared their data with what they believe to be Homer's description of a solar eclipse in *The Odyssey*: "The sun is blotted out from heaven, and a malignant mist has crept upon the world."[3]

They found that there was just one date on which a solar eclipse could have happened during this period: April 16, 1178 BCE. This is in keeping with the time period in which many scholars have placed Homer's story. Even the time of the event—noon—matched up with Homer's description of the sun's position in the sky at the time of its disappearance.

Eclipse

Just like scholars, however, scientists also tend to question one another. Jerry Oltion, a telescope maker and science fiction writer does not think that the *evil mist* was an eclipse. "Any writer who has seen an eclipse—or even heard one described—would never put his characters indoors during the climactic moment,"[4] Oltion said.

Homer is seen here in a section of a fresco titled "Mount Parnassus" by Italian painter Raphael Sanzio (better known as simply Raphael). The work was created on an interior wall of the Stanza della Segnatura in the Vatican Palace.

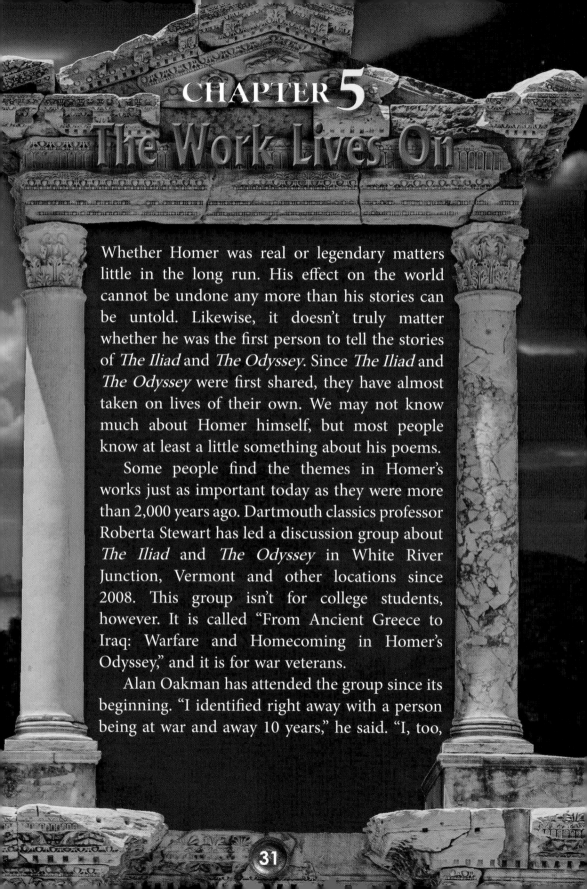

CHAPTER 5
The Work Lives On

Whether Homer was real or legendary matters little in the long run. His effect on the world cannot be undone any more than his stories can be untold. Likewise, it doesn't truly matter whether he was the first person to tell the stories of *The Iliad* and *The Odyssey*. Since *The Iliad* and *The Odyssey* were first shared, they have almost taken on lives of their own. We may not know much about Homer himself, but most people know at least a little something about his poems.

Some people find the themes in Homer's works just as important today as they were more than 2,000 years ago. Dartmouth classics professor Roberta Stewart has led a discussion group about *The Iliad* and *The Odyssey* in White River Junction, Vermont and other locations since 2008. This group isn't for college students, however. It is called "From Ancient Greece to Iraq: Warfare and Homecoming in Homer's Odyssey," and it is for war veterans.

Alan Oakman has attended the group since its beginning. "I identified right away with a person being at war and away 10 years," he said. "I, too, had a wife and child at home while I was in Vietnam. I wanted to survive to get back to see them."[1] At the same time, Oakman points out that coming home from war can lead to many confusing feelings. "You're supposed to be coming back. You're supposed to fit into the piece of the puzzle, kind of smoothly, and everything was supposed to go on as it was before . . . I volunteered for the military, I volunteered for all that, I wasn't angry about it, but I was disillusioned about what it was really all about."[2]

"A Reading from Homer" by Sir Lawrence Alma-Tadema, 1885

By reading Homer's work, Oakman and the other veterans who participate in the program are able to discuss their feelings about war. They also see that they aren't alone. Other members of the group have been dealing with these same life-changing experiences. "That's what Homer and *The Odyssey* do as well," explains Stewart. "They show the problems of deployment and homecoming. Homer is real, in a way. . . . It's a universal story, and it's a universal story that is told really well. It tells us that coming home is as heroic as going out."[3]

The Iliad

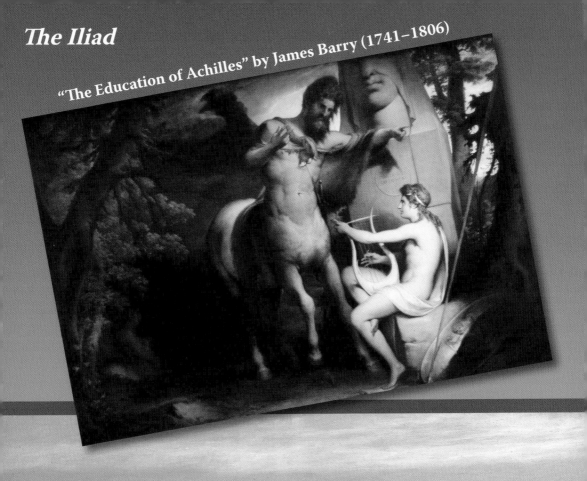

"The Education of Achilles" by James Barry (1741–1806)

"Odysseus and Polyphemus" by Arnold Böcklin (1827–1901)

The Iliad

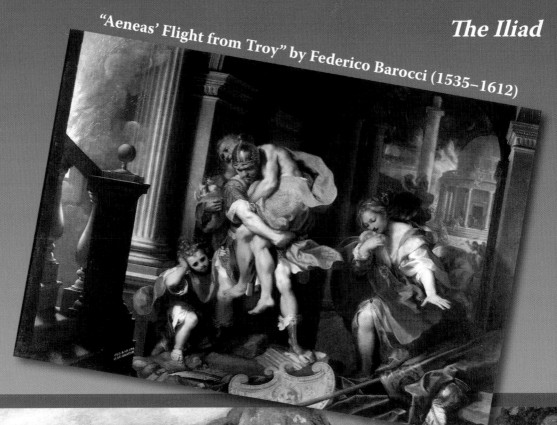

"Aeneas' Flight from Troy" by Federico Barocci (1535–1612)

The Odyssey

Generation after generation of artists, musicians, and writers have used the themes from these works. Some have even inspired one another. The Roman poet Virgil wrote a kind of sequel to *The Iliad* during the first century BCE. His work, called *The Aeneid*, describes the further adventures of the Trojan hero Aeneas. It is also considered a piece of classic literature.

Many artists have depicted scenes from *The Iliad* and *The Odyssey*. One of the first was 16th century German painter Christoph Amberger. Working in the late 18th and early 19th centuries, Swiss painter Henry Fuseli illustrated both *The Iliad* and *The Odyssey*. Poet William Cowper looked to Fuseli's paintings when translating Homer's work into English at about the same time. French sculptor Jean-Auguste Barre, and Italian painter Francesco Hayez were among the 19th century artists who depicted the two poems. African-American artist Romare Bearden did the same thing in the 20th century, depicting Odysseus and other characters as African Americans to show that strength was not limited racially.

Numerous writers around the world have made use of the poems as well. One of the most

Odysseus Marble in Museo Chiaramonti in the Vatican Museum

"Odysseus in Front of
Scylla and Charybdis"
by Henry Fuseli

Roman poet Virgil is seen here reading his work, *The Aeneid*, to Roman emperor Augustus, his wife Livia, and his sister Octavia. Virgil wrote *The Aeneid* as a follow-up to Homer's epic poem *The Iliad*. Themes from both *The Iliad* and *The Odyssey* can be found in Virgil's work. Some say it was his way of competing with the famous bard.

notable was Irish author James Joyce. Joyce retold the story of Odysseus and updated it to Dublin, Ireland in the early 20th century in his novel *Ulysses*, published in 1922. The book is now considered a piece of classic literature in its own right.

Modern television producers and filmmakers have also turned to Homer for inspiration. *Helen of Troy* was the name of both a 1956 movie as well as a 2003 television mini-series about the Trojan War. NBC released a mini-series called *The Odyssey* in 1997. There was also a 1962 Italian film called *Fury of Achilles*. In 2004, Brad Pitt starred as Achilles in *Troy*, the most recent major film about the war.

The 2000 film *O Brother, Where Art Thou?*—which is directed by brothers Ethan and Joel Coen—is said to be a spot-on modern version of *The Odyssey*. Many of the major characters correspond to characters in *The Odyssey*. For example, star George Clooney's character is named Ulysses, the Roman version of Odysseus. John Goodman's "Big Dan" Teague has one eye and corresponds to the Cyclops Polyphemus, Holly Hunter (Penny) is Penelope, and the blind radio station manager Mr. Lund (played by Stephen Root) is meant to be Homer himself. Interestingly, neither of the Coen brothers had read *The Odyssey*, though they were familiar with the story through several adaptations.

While many people dispute where Homer was born, some believe that he died on the island of Ios. This too, of course, is open for debate. Some say that Ios was the home of Homer's mother, a woman named **Clymene**. Just as there is no proof that Homer ever lived, there is likewise no proof of his death. A tomb said to be his final resting place can be found in Plakoto, the northernmost part of the island. Like the lost city of Troy, the mysterious grave lies under a hill.

The Homeria Festival

The people of the Greek Island of Ios have a special place in their hearts for Homer and *The Iliad* and *The Odyssey*. Starting in 1991 and held every May since then, the island has held a festival honoring the poet and his work. The celebration is called the Homeria, and it lasts for three days.

During this time the customary beach-party atmosphere of the island changes. The mood becomes more serious, but the festival is also a fun time for all. The festival draws many people from all over the world. These visitors, along with the locals, attend sporting events, theater productions, lectures, and art exhibits.

The highlight of the Homeria comes on May 15, when the locals carry a flame from the port to the tomb that is believed to be Homer's final resting place. Visitors are encouraged to join in this march. It is meant to honor the poet as well as to bring all the festival attendees, from both near and far, together in their appreciation of him.

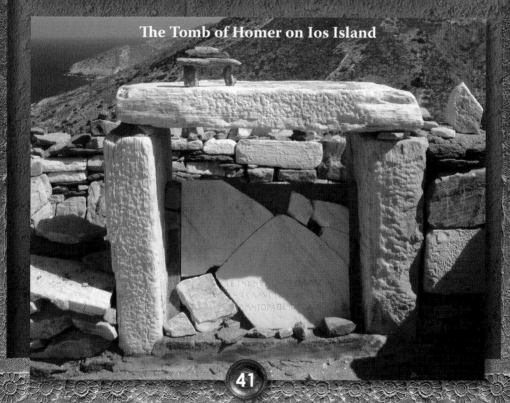

The Tomb of Homer on Ios Island

All Dates BCE and some are approximations

3500	Sumerians migrate from Asia into the region of the Tigris and Euphrates Rivers and establish a flourishing civilization.
3000–1100	The Bronze Age takes place in Greece.
2560	The Great Pyramid of Giza is built in Egypt.
2000–1700	The Mycenaeans enter mainland Greece and establish an important civilization.
1250	The Mycenaean civilization reaches its peak.
1200	The Trojan War takes place.
1178	The solar eclipse—or something similar—mentioned in *The Odyssey* may have happened at this time.
1150–750	The Dark Ages take place in Greece.
1100–1000	Greek colonization of the eastern coast of the Aegean Sea begins.
776	The Olympic Games begin in Olympia, Greece.
ca. 700	Homer composes *The Iliad* and *The Odyssey*.
509	Democracy is introduced in the Greek city-state of Athens.
479	Greeks defeat invading Persian army at the Battle of Plataea and set the stage for the "Golden Age" of Greece.
431	The Peloponnesian War divides Greece and rages for 27 years.
ca. 280	Scholars began suggesting that Homer's poems were written by different people.
29–19	Roman poet Virgil writes *The Aeneid*.

Chapter 1: The Original Action-Adventure Experience

1. Homer, *The Iliad*. Translated by Samuel Butler (Mineola, New York: Dover Publications, 1999), page 1.
2. Robert Steven Bianchi, "Who Was Homer?" *Calliope*, November 1998, Issue 3, page 4.

Chapter 2: More Questions than Answers

1. John Noble Wilford, "Homer's Sea: Wine Dark?" *New York Times*, December 20, 1983. http://www.nytimes.com/1983/12/20/science/homer-s-sea-wine-dark.html
2. Madeline Miller, "My Hero: Homer." *The Guardian*, June 2, 2012. http://www.guardian.co.uk/books/2012/jun/01/my-hero-homer-madeline-miller

Chapter 3: Homer—Man or Legend?

1. John Miles Foley, "'Reading' Homer Through Oral Tradition." *College Literature*, Spring 2007, Volume 34, Issue 2, p. 1.
2. Ibid., p 6.
3. Richard Saltus, "Scholar Says Homer Inspired Greek ABC's, New Theory on Origins of Key Alphabet Draws Questions from Other Classicists." *Boston Globe*, January 11, 1989.

Chapter 4: Mixing Facts with Fiction

1. Stefan Lovgren, "Is Troy True? The Evidence Behind Movie Myth." *National Geographic News*, May 14, 2004. http://news.nationalgeographic.com/news/2004/05/0514_040514_troy.html
2. Ibid.
3. Homer. *The Odyssey*. Translated by E.V. Rieu (New York, New York: Greenwich House, 1982), p. 314.
4. Richard A. Lovett, "Ancient Eclipse Found in '*The Odyssey*,' Scientists Say." *National Geographic News*, June 23, 2008. http://news.nationalgeographic.com/news/2008/06/080623-homer-eclipse.html

Chapter 5: The Works Live On

1. Nicola Smith, "When Soldiers Come Home From War." *Valley News*, May 28, 2011.
2. Ibid.
3. Ibid.

Books

Evslin, Bernard. *The Trojan War* (Kindle Edition). New York: Open Road Young Readers, 2012.

Homer. *The Iliad* (Greek Classics). Adapted by Beatrice Sampatakou. Stroud, Gloustershire, United Kingdom: Real Reads, 2013.

Homer. *The Odyssesy* (Greek Classics). Adapted by Beatrice Sampatakou. Stroud, Gloustershire, United Kingdom: Real Reads, 2013.

Manguel, Alberto. *Homer's The Iliad and The Odyssey: A Biography*. New York: Grove Press, 2009.

Orr, Tamra. *Achilles* (Profiles in Greek and Roman Mythology). Hockessin, DE: Mitchell Lane Publishers, 2008.

Rubalcaba, Jill and Eric Cline. *Digging for Troy: From Homer to Hisarlik*. Watertown, MA: Charlesbridge, 2011.

Tracy, Kathleen. *The Life and Times of Homer*. Hockessin, DE: Mitchell Lane Publishers, 2004.

Tracy, Kathleen. *Odysseus* (Profiles in Greek and Roman Mythology). Hockessin, DE: Mitchell Lane Publishers, 2008.

Works Consulted

Edwards, Mark W. *Homer: Poet of the Iliad*. Baltimore, MD: Johns Hopkins University Press, 1987.

Foley, John Miles. "Reading Homer Through Oral Tradition." *College Literature*, Spring 2007, Volume 34, Issue 2, pages 1–28.

Graziosi, Barbara. *Inventing Homer: The Early Reception of the Epic*. Cambridge, United Kingdom: Cambridge University Press, 2002.

Homer. *The Iliad*. Translated by Samuel Butler. Mineola, New York: Dover Publications, 1999.

On the Internet

Ancient Greece for Kids: Homer's Iliad
http://www.ducksters.com/history/ancient_greece/iliad.php

Ancient Greece for Kids: Homer's Odyssey
http://www.ducksters.com/history/ancient_greece/odyssey.php

FactMonster.com: Trojan War
http://www.factmonster.com/encyclopedia/entertainment/trojan-war.html

History Channel—Trojan War
http://www.history.com/topics/trojan-war

Achaeans (uh-KEE-uhns)

Achilles (uh-KIL-eez)

Agamemnon (aa-guh-MEHM-nahn)

Athena (uh-THEEN-uh)

Briseis (BRIS-ee-uhs)

Calypso (kuh-LIP-soh)

Clymene (CLIH-muh-nee)

Menelaus (mehn-uh-LAY-us)

Odysseus (oh-DEE-see-us)

Poseidon (puh-SI-duhn)

Heinrich Schliemann (HINE-rik SHLEE-mahn)

Tiresias (tur-EE-see-uhs)

Zeus (ZYOOS)

Bust of Homer in the British Museum. Roman copy of a lost Hellenistic original of the 2nd century BC.

GLOSSARY

archaeology (ahr-kee-AWL-uh-jee)—The scientific study of prehistoric peoples and their cultures through their artifacts and other remains.

bard (BAHRD)—A person who composes and recites epic poems, often while playing music.

deploy (dih-PLOI)—To send troops into battle.

dialect (DIE-uh-lekt)—A variety of language that is different from other varieties due to the geography of the speakers.

disillusion (dis-ih-LOO-zhuhn)—To free from an ideal belief.

mnemonic (nih-MAWN-ik)—Something intended to assist in memorization

prosaic (proh-ZAY-ik)—Ordinary to the point of being dull.

suitor (SOO-tuhr)—A man who courts a woman.

syllable (SIHL-uh-buhl)—One or more letters that represent a single sound.